the Living Ocean
Seals
and
Sea Lions

Bobbie Kalman & John Crossingham

Crabtree Publishing Company

www.crabtreebooks.com

Created by Bobbie Kalman

Dedicated by Crystal Foxton
To my grandmother, Alma Whiteman, for the love and laughter you've shown me over the years!

Editor-in-Chief
Bobbie Kalman

Writing team
Bobbie Kalman
John Crossingham

Substantive editor
Kathryn Smithyman

Project editor
Molly Aloian

Editors
Robin Johnson
Kelley MacAulay

Design
Margaret Amy Salter
Samantha Crabtree (cover)

Production coordinator
Heather Fitzpatrick

Photo research
Crystal Foxton

Consultant
Patricia Loesche, Ph.D., Animal Behavior Program,
Department of Psychology, University of Washington

Special thanks to
National Oceanic and Atmospheric Administration/Department of Commerce

Illustrations
Barbara Bedell: pages 5 (all except fur seal), 6 (monk seal), 15, 19, 24-25 (krill, orca, penguin, shark, and squid), 29
Katherine Kantor: pages 6 (ringed seal), 24-25 (leopard seal)
Bonna Rouse: pages 5 (fur seal), 6 (elephant seal), 7, 24-25 (background, Antarctic fur seal, octopus, and Wedell seal)
Margaret Amy Salter: pages 24-25 (herring, magnifying glasses, and plankton)

Photographs
iStockphoto.com: Joe Gough: page 13 (top); Harry Klerks: page 12; Kevin Tate: page 19 (bottom)
National Oceanic and Atmospheric Administration/Department of Commerce: page 31
SeaPics.com: ©Robin W. Baird: pages 23 (top), 30; ©Bob Cranston: page 15; ©Goran Ehlme: page 23 (bottom); ©Florian Graner: page 22; ©Mark J. Rauzon: page 11 (bottom); ©Kevin Schafer: page 21; ©Masa Ushioda: page 13 (bottom)
©Stone, Lynn/Animals Animals - Earth Scenes: page 27
Visuals Unlimited: Brandon Cole: page 29; Charles McRae: page 8 (top)
Other images by Corel, Digital Stock, Digital Vision, Eyewire, and Photodisc

Crabtree Publishing Company

www.crabtreebooks.com   1-800-387-7650

Copyright © **2006 CRABTREE PUBLISHING COMPANY**.
All rights reserved. No part of this publication may be reproduced, stored in a retrieval system or be transmitted in any form or by any means, electronic, mechanical, photocopying, recording, or otherwise, without the prior written permission of Crabtree Publishing Company. In Canada: We acknowledge the financial support of the Government of Canada through the Book Publishing Industry Development Program (BPIDP) for our publishing activities.

Cataloging-in-Publication Data
Kalman, Bobbie.
  Seals and sea lions / Bobbie Kalman & John Crossingham.
       p. cm. -- (The living ocean series)
  Includes index.
  ISBN-13: 978-0-7787-1301-2 (rlb)
  ISBN-10: 0-7787-1301-6 (rlb)
  ISBN-13: 978-0-7787-1323-4 (pbk)
  ISBN-10: 0-7787-1323-7 (pbk)
  1. Seals (Animals)--Juvenile literature. 2. Sea lions--Juvenile literature.
  I. Crossingham, John. II. Title. III. Series.
  QL737.P64K36 2005
  599.79--dc22
                                                        2005022993
                                                           LC

**Published in
the United States**
PMB16A
350 Fifth Ave.
Suite 3308
New York, NY
10118

**Published
in Canada**
616 Welland Ave.,
St. Catharines, Ontario
Canada
L2M 5V6

**Published in the
United Kingdom**
73 Lime Walk
Headington
Oxford
OX3 7AD
United Kingdom

**Published
in Australia**
386 Mt. Alexander Rd.,
Ascot Vale (Melbourne)
VIC 3032

Contents

Seals and sea lions are mammals

Seals and sea lions are **mammals**. Mammals are **warm-blooded** animals, which means their bodies stay about the same temperatures in both hot and cold surroundings. Mammals are also **vertebrates**, or animals with backbones.

Like all mammals, seals and sea lions have body parts called lungs for breathing air. They also have some fur or hair on their bodies. Baby mammals **nurse**, or drink milk from the bodies of their mothers.

Marine mammals

Seals and sea lions belong to a group of mammals called **marine mammals**. Marine mammals live and find food mainly in oceans. Some marine mammals, including seals, sea lions, walruses, and polar bears, live both in oceans and on land. Other marine mammals, such as sea otters, manatees, whales, and dugongs live only in oceans.

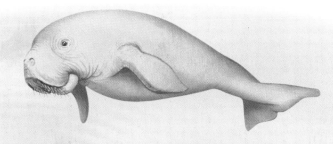

Dugongs live only in oceans. They search the water for ocean plants to eat.

Polar bears have thick fur that keeps them warm both on land and in water.

Three family groups

Most scientists believe that seals and sea lions belong to an **order**, or group, of marine mammals called **pinnipeds**. There are three family groups of pinnipeds. One family is known as "earless seals." This family is made up of seals that are also known as "true seals." Another family is called "eared seals." It is made up of fur seals and sea lions. Walruses make up the third family of pinnipeds.

A monk seal is an earless seal.

A sea lion is an eared seal.

A fur seal is an eared seal.

A walrus is related to seals and sea lions.

So many species!

There are about eighteen **species**, or types, of earless seals and about sixteen species of eared seals known today. These pages show some of these species. Earless seals and eared seals have similar bodies.

Earless seals

Earless seals have ears, but they do not have **ear flaps**. Ear flaps are pieces of skin that cover the ears.

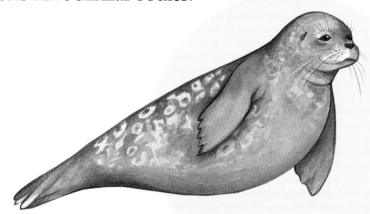

The ringed seal gets its name from the small, ringlike markings on its body.

Female monk seals are larger than male monk seals are. A female can be up to eight feet (2.4 m) long. A male Hawaiian monk seal can be up to seven feet (2.1 m) long.

*The **southern** elephant seal is one of the largest seal species. A male southern elephant seal can weigh up to 6,600 pounds (2994 kg). This seal gets its name from its large size and big nose.*

Eared seals

There are about nine species of fur seals and about five species of sea lions in the eared seal family. Both fur seals and sea lions have ear flaps that cover their ears.

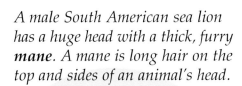

The California sea lion is often seen along the shores of California.

The Antarctic fur seal is one of the few species of eared seals that lives in cold places. It has thick fur covering its body.

A male South American sea lion has a huge head with a thick, furry **mane**. *A mane is long hair on the top and sides of an animal's head.*

The largest fur seals are the South African fur seal, shown above, and the Australian fur seal. These seals look almost identical.

*One species of earless seal lives in **fresh water**. The small baikal seal lives in Lake Baikal, which is in Russia.*

This Australian sea lion lives near the southern coast of Australia.

Seals and sea lions live in **saltwater** oceans all over the world. Most species of earless seals live in cold **polar oceans**. Most species of eared seals live in **temperate oceans**. Temperate oceans are found in parts of the world where the seasons change. These oceans are warm in summer and cold in winter. A few species of seals and sea lions live in warm **tropical oceans**. Tropical oceans are located near the **equator**, where the weather is warm year round.

At home in the range

The area in which a seal or sea lion lives, finds food, and has **pups**, or babies, is called a **home range**. The home ranges of most species of seals and sea lions are in **coastal waters**, or waters located near land. Some species of seals and sea lions live in the open oceans far from shores.

Small range, large range

Some species of seals and sea lions have small home ranges. These species live and find food in one particular part of an ocean year round. Hawaiian monk seals have small home ranges. Other species of seals and sea lions have large home ranges. Their home ranges are large because these animals **migrate**. To migrate means to travel long distances to a new area for a certain period of time. For example, from November to March, northern fur seals live and feed in open oceans. In April, they migrate north to have pups.

A big haul

Although they live and find food in oceans, all species of seals and sea lions must leave the water to give birth to pups. They also leave the water to escape from **predators**, to rest, and to **bask**, or lie in the sun and warm their bodies. Leaving the water is called **hauling out**. Seals and sea lions that live in coastal waters haul out onto the land along the coasts. Species that live in open oceans haul out onto remote islands. Some species migrate to cold oceans that have huge sheets of floating ice, called **pack ice**. These animals haul out onto the ice.

Northern elephant seals migrate farther than do any other seals or sea lions. For most of the year, they live in the northern part of the Pacific Ocean, which is their main feeding area. They migrate thousands of miles to have their babies on land in California.

This California sea lion is basking in the sun on a sandy beach.

Body basics

The bodies of seals and sea lions are designed for swimming and diving. Their muscular bodies are **streamlined**, or sleekly shaped, which helps the animals move quickly through water. All seals and sea lions have two front flippers and two **hind**, or back, flippers for swimming. Both seals and sea lions have long, sensitive whiskers that help them feel their way in dark waters. Seals and sea lions have nostrils that they close when they dive into water.

An earless seal

*An earless seal uses its hind flippers only when it swims. Its toes are **webbed** for extra pushing power. Webbed toes have skin between them.*

nostrils

whiskers

Some earless seals have claws on their front flippers. The seals use their claws to drag themselves across land.

Full of fat

All seals and sea lions have some **blubber**, or fat, on their bodies. Most species of earless seals have thick blubber that traps heat inside their bodies. The blubber is between 2.8 and 4 inches (7.1-10.2 cm) thick.

Fine fur

Earless seals have short, fine fur on their bodies. Many hairs grow out of each **follicle**, or opening on the skin from which hair grows. The fur grows in clumps. Every year, earless seals leave the water to **molt**, or shed, clumps of fur.

An eared seal

ear flap

Eared seals are able to turn their hind flippers forward. Earless seals cannot turn their hind flippers forward.

The fur of eared seals is thicker than the fur of earless seals.

Eared seals do not have claws on their front flippers.

male
female

Nice coat

Both sea lions and fur seals have thick fur. The fur covers every part of their bodies, except their flippers and parts of their faces. Fur seals have fur made up of two layers of hair. The first layer, called the **underhair**, is thick, soft hair. The underhair is dense and oily. The oil **repels**, or keeps away, water. The second layer of hair is made up of long, stiff hairs called **guard hairs**. The guard hairs trap a layer of air over the underhair. This combination of trapped air and oily hair keeps water away from the skin. Although the fur is thick, each hair grows separately from a single follicle. As a result, fur seals lose their hair gradually throughout the year, rather than all at once.

Male eared seals are much bigger than the females of the same species. The male South American sea lion, shown on the left, is much bigger than the female is.

Different flippers

Both on land and in water, eared seals move their flippers differently than earless seals do. Eared seals are able to turn their hind flippers forward. Turning their hind flippers forward allows eared seals to "walk" on land using all four flippers.

Earless seals cannot move their hind flippers forward. On land, earless seals use only their front flippers to drag their bodies forward.

On ice, earless seals slide forward by moving their bodies up and down in a rippling motion.

Earless seals push

Earless seals swim by moving their hind flippers from side to side. This motion pushes the seals quickly through water. These seals do not often use their front flippers to swim. Instead, they keep their front flippers flat against the sides of their bodies. Earless seals sometimes hold their front flippers out to the sides, which helps the seals balance as they swim.

Eared seals flap

Fur seals and sea lions have long, sleek front flippers that look similar to wings. These animals swim by flapping their front flippers up and down in water. Eared seals have strong shoulder and neck muscles. They use these muscles to move their front flippers. Eared seals do not use their hind flippers for swimming or for steering their bodies through water.

This New Zealand fur seal turns its hind flippers forward as it moves on land.

*The California sea lion swims using two main strokes. During the **power stroke**, the sea lion spreads its front flippers wide and turns them to push against the water. During the **recovery stroke**, the sea lion turns its front flippers flat against its body. This stroke allows the sea lion to move smoothly through water.*

Diving dynamos

Differences in diving

Hawaiian monk seals are mainly shallow divers. They dive between 32 and 131 feet (9.8-39.9 m). Their dives last from three to six minutes. Weddell seals dive under ice in the Southern Ocean. They may dive between 40 and 50 times in an hour while looking for food. They dive 164 to 1,640 feet (50-500 m) deep. Northern elephant seals can dive to depths of 1,148 to 1,312 feet (350-400 m) and spend an average of 20 to 30 minutes under water during each dive.

A leopard seal makes shallow, short dives to look for food.

Seals and sea lions are great divers. They dive to find food and to escape from predators. Most species of earless seals dive deeper and for longer periods of time than most species of eared seals do. Some species of earless seals stay in the ocean, making dive after dive for weeks or months at a time. Adult seals and sea lions can dive for longer periods of time and can dive deeper than young seals and sea lions can.

Up for air

Seals and sea lions must swim to the surface to breathe air. Sea lions usually take only one breath each time they come up for air. Both earless seals and fur seals remain at the surface to take several breaths between dives. Species that stay in the ocean for long periods of time sleep under water. Some species rest under water in holes they find in rocks or ice. They rise to the surface to breathe and then sink back down without waking up! Parts of their brains stay awake to control their breathing while the animals are asleep.

Under pressure

The ocean presses against the bodies of underwater animals from all sides. This pressure is called **water pressure**. Water pressure increases with depth. Before you go under water in a pool, the last thing you do is take a deep breath. Before a seal dives, however, it actually empties the air from its lungs. Air is lighter than water. As the seal dives deep, the heavy weight of the water around it causes pressure on its body. If its lungs were full of light air, they would be crushed by the water pressure.

Storing oxygen

Seals and sea lions do not hold their breath while they are under water. Instead, they store **oxygen** in their blood and muscles. Blood always flows to their hearts and brains, but during long dives, some **organs** in seals and sea lions temporarily shut down. Having bodies that shut down organs, such as the liver or kidneys, helps seals and sea lions conserve oxygen and allows them to dive for longer periods of time.

This northern elephant seal can dive to depths at which humans could not survive!

Super senses

Sounds, light, and scents all move differently through water than they move through air. Since seals and sea lions live both in water and on land, their senses must work well in both places.

Bright eyes

Water near the surface of an ocean can be bright, but deep waters are dark. Seals and sea lions have large eyes that let in as much light as possible. At the back of their eyes, these animals have layers of **membranes** called **tapeta**. The tapeta send the light that enters the eyes back through the eyes a second time. As a result, the amount of light entering the eyes is doubled. Double the amount of light allows the animals to see even in low light. On land, the **pupils** of seals and sea lions become tiny. Tiny pupils limit the amount of light that enters the eyes.

This seal uses its large eyes to see both under water and on land.

Hear, hear!

Seals and sea lions have excellent hearing—both in and out of the water. Under water, it is difficult to know the direction from which a sound comes. Seals and sea lions have bones in their ears that help these animals locate sounds. While hunting, seals and sea lions follow sounds in order to find **prey**. Prey are animals that are eaten by predators. Seals and sea lions also use their excellent hearing to locate one another and their pups.

Smell you later!

Seals and sea lions do not use their sense of smell to find food in water. On land, however, their sense of smell is important. Each animal has a different scent, so a group of seals and sea lions can recognize one another by their smells. For example, a mother knows the scent of her pup and sniffs the air to locate it in a crowd. Certain smells also tell males that females are ready to **mate**, or join together to make babies.

This mother and pup can identify each other by their scents.

Rookeries

Seals and sea lions are among the few marine mammals that mate and have pups on land or ice. In water, most species of seals and sea lions live alone or in small groups. During **mating season**, however, they haul out in huge groups called **rookeries**. Mothers are safer from ocean predators when they are out of the water. Rookeries contain many seals and sea lions, so the animals are also safe from land predators while they are mating and having pups.

Rookeries on land

Many species of seals and sea lions haul out onto land. Most species, including Steller sea lions, form rookeries on islands because there are fewer land predators on islands than there are on **mainlands**. Other species, such as the South African fur seals shown above, form rookeries both on islands and on mainlands.

Some land rookeries contain thousands of females. To stay safe, a few animals watch for predators and warn the others when there is danger nearby.

Rookeries on ice

Most species of earless seals form rookeries on ice. Three species—Weddell seals, baikal seals, and ringed seals—form rookeries on **fast ice**. Fast ice is thick ice that is attached to land. Other earless seals haul out onto pack ice to form rookeries. Pack ice is formed from large pieces of floating and drifting ice.

Meeting to mate

Male fur seals and sea lions and the males of a few species of earless seals are larger than the females of the species are. Male southern elephant seals are up to ten times as large as female southern elephant seals! Two huge males may fight each other for a chance to mate with a female. The strongest males mate with the females.

Rookeries on pack ice are smaller than other rookeries are. Pack ice is neither as large nor is as stable as land or fast ice.

A fight between two male elephant seals is loud and tough. The seals lift up their bodies and bash their heads and chests against each other to prove their strength. At the end of the fight, both seals are cut and scratched.

Make some noise!

Seals and sea lions send messages to one another by **vocalizing**, or making sounds using their voices. These sounds are common in rookeries. Males make loud grunts and roars while mating to scare other males away. Both males and females make high-pitched calls to warn others when predators are nearby.

Capable pups

Most seal and sea lion pups are able to move and **communicate**, or send messages, as soon as they are born. Harbor seal pups are able to swim just one hour after they are born! They often swim alongside their mothers.

No time to waste!

Earless seal pups that live on pack ice nurse only for about two weeks. Their mothers produce milk that helps the pups grow quickly. The milk is fatty and full of **nutrients**, so the pups gain blubber quickly. For example, in just nine days, a harp seal pup can grow from 24 pounds (10.8 kg) to 75 pounds (34 kg)! The mother seals must soon **wean**, or gradually stop feeding, their pups. The mothers wean their babies after a short time because the pack ice on which they nurse is constantly breaking up. While their pups nurse, earless seal mothers **fast**, or stop eating, and live off the energy in their blubber. Once the pups are weaned, the mothers leave them to hunt. The pups begin swimming and **foraging**, or looking for food, on their own.

Mother seals and sea lions usually give birth to only one pup at a time. A newborn pup's eyes open right after it is born, and the pup makes sounds to tell its mother that it needs food.

Lazy summer days

Mother fur seals and sea lions and earless seals that live in warm places spend extra time feeding their pups. Most seal pups are weaned in about four to six weeks. Sea lion pups nurse for six to eleven months. Galapagos fur seal pups nurse for two to three years! Unlike most seal mothers, fur seal and sea lion mothers do not fast while their pups are nursing. They do not have enough body fat to fast.

These mothers feed the pups for a few days and then leave their pups to find food in the ocean. The young pups fast while their mothers are gone. After feeding for several days, the mothers return to the pups so the pups can nurse again. As the pups grow, they learn how to find food for themselves. The mother fur seals and sea lions spend longer and longer periods of time feeding in the ocean, until they no longer feed their pups at all.

A mother harp seal lies on her side while her pup nurses.

Who's hungry?

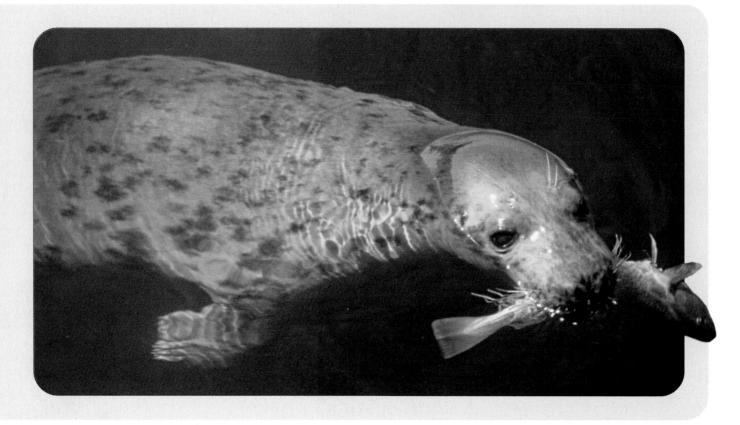

Seals and sea lions are predators. Each seal and sea lion species hunts and eats different prey. Most species eat a wide variety of prey, including octopuses, fish, crabs, clams, squids, shrimps, and penguins. Certain species of seals and sea lions, such as southern fur seals and Steller sea lions, also eat other seals and sea lions. To find prey, some species of seals and sea lions make a number of dives into the water. These groups of dives are called **dive bouts**. While they are under water, seals and sea lions search for food. They swim to the surface for short periods of time between dives. Most seals and sea lions have sharp teeth for grabbing food, but they do not chew their food. Instead, seals and sea lions swallow their food whole or tear it into chunks.

Crabeater seal

The crabeater seal feeds on tiny, shrimplike animals called **krill**. These seals have special teeth that help them strain food from water. First, a crabeater seal sucks water and krill into its mouth. It then clamps its teeth shut and pushes the water out of its mouth. As the water leaves the seal's mouth, the krill get caught between the seal's teeth. The seal then swallows its meal.

A leopard seal, shown above, feeds on krill, penguins, fish, and the pups of other seal species. A leopard seal's teeth are not sharp enough to bite through the flesh of its prey, however. Instead, the seal grabs its prey and shakes it until the prey's flesh comes loose.

Part of the web

To stay alive, every animal must eat plants or other animals. When animals eat, they receive energy. A **food chain** is the pattern of living things eating and being eaten. Energy is passed from one living thing to another through food. When an animal from one food chain eats an animal from another food chain, the two food chains connect. Connected food chains form **food webs**. In the food web shown below, the arrows point toward the living things that are receiving energy. For example, the web shows that penguins eat herring, and that orcas and leopard seals eat penguins.

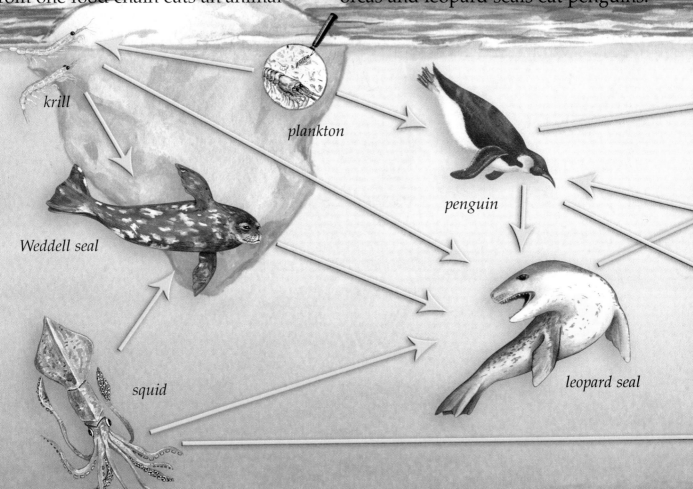

krill

plankton

penguin

Weddell seal

squid

leopard seal

Everything is connected

All living things in a food web are connected. The connections help create an **ecosystem**. An ecosystem is made up of all the living and non-living things in an area. Animals, plants, rocks, ice, and even the water itself are all part of ocean ecosystems. Seals and sea lions help the ecosystems in which they live by eating weak or sick animals. Hunting these animals keeps animal populations strong and healthy, because the weakest animals are removed. Seals and sea lions are also important sources of food for predators. Predators such as polar bears, orcas, and sharks all feed on seals and sea lions.

orca

krill

plankton

octopus

herring

Antarctic fur seal

shark

A history of hunting

This hunter has caught a seal, which will provide food for him and his family.

Native people, such as the Inuit, have been hunting seals and sea lions for thousands of years. Seals and sea lions provide these people with food, fuel, and clothing. Hunting that provides people with the food and supplies they need to survive is called **subsistence hunting**. Subsistence hunting is not wasteful because the hunters use almost every part of the animals they catch.

Commercial hunting

For many centuries, **commercial** hunters have hunted seals and sea lions to make money. Commercial hunters killed huge numbers of seals and sea lions for their blubber, which was made into soap or other materials. They also killed seals for their **pelts**, or fur-covered skins. The pelts were sold and made into fur coats. Commercial hunting is wasteful because the hunters take only the parts they can sell and leave the rest.

In the past, many commercial hunters killed newborn seals. Their pelts sold for a lot of money.

All caught up

Today, people who operate **fisheries** often hunt seals and sea lions. They hunt the animals to stop them from eating too many fish. Some fishery operators even place poisoned **bait** in areas where seals and sea lions feed in order to kill the animals.

Hunting bans

Today, most countries have placed limits on the number of seals and sea lions that people can hunt.

In some areas, the hunting of seals and sea lions is **banned**, or forbidden. Some people break this rule and continue to hunt seals and sea lions, however. Bans have also been placed on the commercial fishing industry. For example, fishing boats are no longer allowed to use certain types of fishing nets. The banned nets once caught seals, sea lions, and other animals as **bycatch**. Bycatch are animals that are accidentally caught in nets intended to catch other animals.

Seals and sea lions sometimes get caught in fishing nets. The animals are either injured, or they drown. Those that survive may have scars for the rest of their lives.

Seals and sea lions in danger

Several species of seals and sea lions have been unable to adjust to recent changes in their **habitats**. A habitat is the natural place where an animal lives. People harm the environment, which destroys both the land and ocean habitats used by seals and sea lions.

Dirty water

Ocean pollution kills seals and sea lions. Ships leak oil, gasoline, and other harmful chemicals into oceans. Harmful fumes from oil spills can also kill seals and sea lions. When people use **pesticides**, chemicals called organochlorine compounds end up in oceans and get absorbed into the bodies of ocean animals. When seals and sea lions eat fish or other animals that have the chemicals in their bodies, they get sick. The chemicals make seals and sea lions **sterile**, or unable to have babies. When seals and sea lions cannot have pups, they cannot add to their populations. As a result, the populations of seals and sea lions slowly decrease.

After an oil spill, seals and sea lions, such as this harbor seal, swim through the oil when they surface to breathe. The oil irritates their eyes, nostrils, and skin.

Endangered species

Despite worldwide bans on hunting, some seal and sea lion species have low populations. Many species are **endangered**. Endangered animals are at risk of dying out in their habitats. **Habitat destruction** is the main cause of the decline in seal and sea lion populations. Both species of monk seals—the Mediterranean monk seal and the Hawaiian monk seal—are endangered. Steller sea lions are also endangered. Scientists are concerned that the populations of several species of fur seals are declining, as well. These animals may soon become endangered.

Slow-growing populations

A seal or sea lion mother gives birth to only one pup each year. As a result, the populations of these animals grow slowly. When hunting, pollution, and habitat destruction kill many seals and sea lions, the number of females having pups gets smaller. Some pups do not grow to be adults to have babies of their own. As a result, several species of seals and sea lions may become endangered.

*Not long ago, there was a third species of monk seal, called the Caribbean monk seal. It is now **extinct**, or no longer found on Earth.*

*Another reason that monk seals and Steller sea lions, shown above, are endangered is that people **overfish** the prey animals that these marine mammals hunt. To overfish means to take too many of one animal from a certain area of water.*

Saving lives

Scientists study seals and sea lions to learn more about how these animals live. They also try to count the animals to learn whether or not their populations are declining. Scientists usually study and count seals and sea lions at rookery sites. It is easier to count seals and sea lions and observe their behavior when the animals are on land or ice.

Tagged for science

The feeding habits of deep-diving seals and sea lions are difficult to observe. Scientists use **tags** to study these animals. A tag is a **radio transmitter** that collects information. The information helps scientists discover how deep, how long, and how many times an animal dives.

Tags help scientists gather information about seals and sea lions as the animals dive in remote places.

Population protection

Scientists often work together with governments to protect seals, sea lions, and other marine mammals. Scientists and governments have developed laws, such as the Marine Mammal Protection Act (MMPA). The MMPA bans hunting, protects rookeries, and prevents people from trading marine mammal products. People around the world also work together to create **marine sanctuaries**. Marine sanctuaries are areas of oceans and land where the activities of people are restricted. The Galapagos Marine Reserve is a marine sanctuary within Galapagos National Park. The reserve was established by the government of Ecuador. Galapagos fur seals and Galapagos sea lions are just two of the species that are protected within this sanctuary.

These Galapagos sea lions live within the Galapagos Marine Reserve in Ecuador.

Glossary

Note: Boldfaced words that are defined in the text may not appear in the glossary.

bait Food or other items that are used to catch birds, fish, or other animals

commercial Describing work that is done to make money

equator The imaginary line around the center of the earth

fishery The industry that catches and sells fish and other marine animals

fresh water Water that does not contain salt, such as the water in a lake or river

habitat destruction The destruction of a natural place where an animal or a plant lives

mainland The main area of land that makes up a continent

mating season The time of year during which animals join together to make babies

membrane A thin layer of body tissue

nutrients Natural substances that help animals grow and develop

organ A part of the body that does an important job, such as the lungs

oxygen A gas that is part of air and water, which plants and animals need to breathe

pesticide A chemical that is used to kill insects

polar ocean A cold ocean that is located at the North Pole or at the South Pole

population The total number of one species of animal living in a particular area

predator An animal that hunts and eats other animals

pupil The black, circular opening in the center of an eye through which light passes

radio transmitter A piece of equipment that allows scientists to track animals

salt water Water that contains salt

Index

1 2 3 4 5 6 7 8 9 0 Printed in the U.S.A. 4 3 2 1 0 9 8 7 6 5